BLACK

A Misunderstood Race

A

Memoir

By

Mansa Mnēmē

"Navigating America in black skin"

© 2018 by M.B. A.K.A Mansa Mnēmē

First published by Verengai Publishing House

07/04/2018

ISBN-978-0-9995371-3-8

VERENGAI PUBLISHING
HOUSE

"The Black skin is not a badge of shame, but rather a glorious symbol of national greatness."

- Marcus Garvey

Contents

Disclaimer 1

This is a book that talks about race in America as seen through the author's eyes. She references black as a term representing all minority groups and references white as a term representing races that do not consider themselves as minorities. This explanation is being provided so that readers understand that every race has been highlighted under two dominating captions and that the author is sensitive to all races.

When the author references "black," she is not representing the feelings, emotions and or thought patterns of all blacks and or minority groups. When the author references "white," she is not representing the actions, feelings, emotions and or thought patterns of all non-blacks and/or whites.

However, to maintain the flow of the book, the author mentions "black" and "white." We trust that we all understand the terms as earlier presented so, happy reading!

Introduction 2

"No one is born hating another person because of the color of his skin, or his background, or his religion. People must learn to hate, and if they can learn to hate, they can be taught to love, for love comes more naturally to the human heart than its opposite."–Nelson Mandela

His name is Jaxyon (I believe that's the spelling his grandmother stated because I remember it being unique). He was two years old at the time… the tallest two-year-old I had ever seen, yet the most adorable one. His eyes were big and round, they reminded me of an Anime character. His cheeks were so cute and slightly chubby.

You should've seen the curls in the boy's hair! He had a head full of adorable strawberry blonde curls. On this day, he wore a red shirt, little black sweatpants, and sneakers. I was working for a mobile healthcare company, where I served as a manager and clinician. Jaxyon and his grandparents were the last ones on our schedule that day, so by the time they came in, I was winding up my front desk process. Once Jaxyon's grandfather completed his paperwork, the clinicians called him back, while Jaxyon's grandmother tried everything to keep this ambitious two-year-old boy busy. He kept escaping and running my way every chance, he got, and I couldn't help but occasionally stop what I was doing to engage this little handsome fellow. Jaxyon's grandparents looked young enough to be his parents (at least to me). At first, I thought they were his parents until his grandmother started talking about her daughter, Jaxyon's mother. With every step I took to pack up, Jaxyon was by my side, talking baby talk, and I, of course, engaging in baby and adult talk as if I understood his language.

I recall trying to pack some electronics in the box and Jaxyon trying his best to help, with scooting the tote. His grandmother was concerned that he was in my way, but I assured her he was doing no harm. It was so cute how he would walk forward when I walked forward. He had long neglected his grandmother, treating her like she was a stranger, and every time she tried to call him, he wouldn't even look her way.

She would chuckle in the background. She mentioned that I must be special because he never really gravitates towards anyone—at all. I remember walking away from my desk for a brief moment, then walking onto the floor only to be treated to a two-year-old bolting my way with open arms! Now, that was kind of cute. I knew instantly that he was coming in for a hug and the international sign of *"pick me up,"* so, I reacted accordingly. I bent forward and grabbed him underneath his arms, picked him up and raised him above my head, finding myself in child's play, with Jaxyon of course, loving every moment, giggling and clapping.

After that brief moment, I tried to put him down, but you can already imagine he would not have it! The moaning began. I literally had to finish packing up my station with him on my hip, and that didn't bother me one bit, especially since he was having a jolly good time, talking away in baby language, and I, of course once—again validating him. His grandmother tried peeling him out of my arms, but Jaxyon wouldn't budge! It was hilarious. She walked away shaking her head; she just couldn't believe how easily he had taken to a stranger like me. She continued to remind me that he was not usually that friendly, while I, of course, was simply a baby whisperer (wink-wink).

Once Jaxyon's grandfather was completely done, it was time for us to part ways, and expectedly, our goodbyes were not easy. His grandmother came to get him out of my hands, but he put up a good fight, one that tickled my heart. Once she grabbed him, it was like he was being stolen; his chubby little fingers reached my way while his face was consumed with tears. I could hear the soundtrack to the Titanic playing in the background, and everything going in slow motion as I waved goodbye to my newly found friend. He did the world's most adorable thing right before they walked out the door— he blew me a kiss, Y'all! I pretended to catch it and place it on my heart. What a moment!

So, a little backstory. In my career, we predominantly serviced rural mid-America, had tons of great conversations with our farmers and small-town folk, and this particular day, it was a town that was out a way from the urban cities—that is. I am pretty sure the black population was less than one percent if there was any in this town. Jaxyon was white.

That meant he had no inkling that I was different. He had no idea that I was "Black," dark and rich in Melanin. He had no idea that I was an *"Nigger."* He was not intimidated or scared of me; he didn't feel unsafe…so where do the adults get it from? Anyway, I digress. Jaxyon saw a human being in me as I, in him. How come we cannot live like this in the west? I had to give you a little backstory to register the fact that the kid most likely hadn't been around any black people so that no one makes an excuse as to why he gravitated towards me.

So, how did he embrace me so tightly? His own grandmother stated time and time again that he did not gravitate towards strangers that easily. It's simple…children are born into the world innocent. They do not have any prejudices ingrained in them. It's the environment and those around them that project their own differences onto them and teach them to be divided. They become subject to the forced opinions of the adults they are around; after all, children are by-products of the environment they come from.

The Beginning 3

"One isn't necessarily born with courage, but one is born with potential. Without courage, we cannot practice any other virtue with consistency. We can't be kind, true, merciful, generous, or honest." —Maya Angelou

I was born and raised in a country in the continent of Africa. I obtained all of my earlier education within my country of birth. Both my parents were raised in the villages of this African Country. (Yes… huts with thatched straw roofs, pretty much what you see on Discovery channel). They grew up in two opposite ends of the country. My father was born and raised in a small mining village that sits West of an unofficial world wonder, and my mother was born and raised North East of the capitol city in a town that sits close to an ancient African Jewish tribe. (urban legend has it that they were the keepers of the Ark of the covenant—who am I to argue?)

My parents grew up during the independence war era, where the locals where fighting the British government so that the natives could reclaim full ownership of their land, free from colonialism. During that time my parents vaguely talked about the treatment by the British colonizers. What I recall is that before independence, they had curfews, and blacks couldn't be in town at a certain time. Blacks couldn't work certain jobs that the British people had, even though

10

they were qualified as well. (Sound familiar?)

My father highlighted his difficulties as a black man in his own country when it came to landing the ultimate career. He talked about discrimination and some challenges he faced especially before independence. That's why the people rose up and fought to get their country back. While growing up, our history books never detailed the discrimination and prejudices, because we learned via a British system. After independence, my parents began to share different positive stories and experiences. My siblings and I were born after the independence. We are considered as the *Born-free Generation,* meaning we were born free from all the prejudices and discrimination that my parents had experienced.

My parents were now able to purchase homes anywhere, and I was born and raised in suburbia. Before independence, there were segregated areas where whites only lived, while the blacks lived in the poorer areas. Even though my parents have shared bits and pieces of their own experiences during the Colonial British regime, they never once called white people out, neither did they ever mention any hate to us about how they were treated.

They never once expressed any strong emotions about it; matter-of-fact, they never really spoke of it unless we asked. I mention that, so you can understand that my parents were not trotting around the house complaining, or saying distasteful things about the British or "white" people.

My siblings and I attended both public and private schools; my brother and sister went to boarding school, and I went to a public school, mainly because I wanted to be with my best friend from primary school. I would have been in someone's dorm otherwise. We participated in all kinds of sports. I played tennis, basketball, and was also on the swimming team. I loved hurdles, ran relays, and participated in the long and short jump. In my school, we had Cubans, Indians, Asians, Angolans, Botswanans, and South Africans, both white and black. We had kids from Europe and the U.S, (mainly children of diplomats) and not to mention we had white Africans. I was exposed to different cultures from a very young age which allowed me to see all people as human beings, and also made me discover that we are all alike in some way.

While growing up, my parents never taught us about the differences of race… they never talked about race or skin. In fact, my mother was a prime example of international diversity as she was well traveled, with friends who were Indians, Ugandans, South Africans and people of several other races. All I knew was that she would introduce these women that didn't look like us, as our aunts (my mother!) She would say, "say hello to Auntie X or Y…" In my culture, your parents' friends are aunts and uncles, and as children, we would just go along with it! My favorite parts of this were the treats they brought us; the samosa, chapati and chicken veggie curry rice… Honey! You have not lived until you acculturate your taste buds.

Therefore, I grew up in a society in which I didn't know about racism and didn't know that there were other races that considered themselves "better" than or "superior" to others, because all my life I was around prominent black people and a small percentage of diverse races which never claimed supremacy. Heck! We didn't even claim black power. (Insert a laughing out loud emoji!) Because the majority population was black, and we knew it.

Denial 4

"The truth has become an insult."— *Chimamanda Ngozi Adichie*

Fast forward to when my family began to migrate, as my mother found it suitable to relocate the family to the west. We as children had no say, so of course, I was 16 years old, when I received the news at that time, and I was not thrilled. I had my group of friends, we had our maids, gardeners and a unique lifestyle. Life was good for me, (or so I thought) so why would we want to move? My mother insisted that if we wanted to stay, we could, but we would have no one with us because the entire family will be gone. I was a teenager, and I just wasn't ready to depart, but needless to say, we all did. My mother had already been living in the U.S.A, so by the time we arrived in the west, she had schools picked out. She gave us the "speech;" we had arrived in the land of *"milk and honey,"* (using those exact words by the way), so what we made out of this sacrifice was our choice.

She then continued by telling us about the drug pandemic and cautioned us about going down that road, as well as many other roads. Did I mention that I didn't even know what "drugs" were at this time?! Anyways, what struck me was that during this great speech, she never mentioned race. My guess is that we were settling in Southern California, a very racially diverse community and my mother had probably not experienced any racial mistreatment.

My oldest brother and I got thrown into the busy high school system of America, where information overload, mixed with tons of culture shock had us exchanging our experiences into the wee hours of the night. Having thick accents didn't help my brother and me, and for months, the kids would ask, some out of fascination and some out of ignorance, several medieval questions about Africa, our pet lions, if we rode elephants and all that. Some would even ask if we only started wearing clothes when we arrived to the west! Out of frustration, my clever older brother told me, "do what I do." I asked him what that was, and he said he just plays along with them; he just went with the flow of whatever stupid question or comment they sent his way.

I tried it because I'd also grown tired of explaining to people that I grew up in the "burbs" (suburban area) in Africa, and that we actually had a certain accustomed lifestyle that consisted of drivers that took us to school and picked us up, maids and gardeners, not to forget big homes with swimming pools, and the whole nine yards. But no one wanted to hear that. People wanted to hear the Discovery channel stories, so I played along like my brother said, and never got hackled again (weird how that works.) My experiences in high school grew better with time, as more white students gravitated my way, most out of fascination, although you could sense their sincerity. The really weird part was that the few black students that crossed my path literally avoided me.

(I will continue this in detail in subject: Dear Black People). Anyway, I ended up hanging out with the African students, not by choice, but by comfort, since they embraced me because we were all from Africa. In that circle was one sweet, kind African American girl (just one!) Bless her heart for being different.

Southern California was pretty cool. I didn't feel any type of way in terms of racial discrimination or prejudices. Needless to say, my western onboarding was a different experience. I had my first little part-time job in Southern California in a racially diverse environment, so much that I learned communicative Spanish. I was never concerned about having black skin, as we lived in the valley, away from big metropolitan cities, which was great, but not so great, as it was there that I think my naivety was born.

I remember going to a prominent University campus in Riverside California with my friend and overhearing a group of young black men lost in a debate. My curiosity was piqued, so I stood close by to hear what their public debacle was all about, and for the first time, I heard a conversation about the "white man." My friend tried to grab my hand, but I was too interested. Besides I had given her a ride so she could register for classes, so I simply told her I would be right there when she got back.

There were about five guys animatedly saying the same thing but offering different opinions about the "white man." So, foolishly, I just jumped in, "You shouldn't blame anything on anyone, whatever you want you can get in life." Boy! Did that stop them in their tracks, as they all turned my way and let me have it!

16

I had no facts and no idea how black people in America felt. Heck, I didn't even know that my brothers and sisters were products of slavery until my junior year of high school. The British educational system did NOT teach us that part in the African country in which I grew up, for obvious reasons. The boys argued that a black man had to get two degrees more than his white counterpart to get the same job. They were not mean in their response to me, but they gave me a breakdown of African American history from their experience in less than five minutes, and frankly speaking, I still didn't get it.

No one in my life had ever depicted another race as being a "full-stop" to what anyone could become. My parents had indeed experienced discrimination, but I guess the difference was that a solution was eventually provided in the form of independence, after which my parents didn't have any race issues hindering their path to a successful life. So, I certainly couldn't process the idea the boys were so desperately trying to convey.

.

Being Black in America 5

"The black skin in America comes with a target mark, and to be marked is to be hunted."— Mansa Mnēmē

The first time I realized I was black in America was when I moved to Missouri in the Mid-west. It was a rude awakening. After high school, prior to moving to the Mid-West, some black Americans had exhausted time "trying" to tell me about racism and black injustice, but I couldn't see it. I'd always tell them that maybe when it blatantly happened before my eyes, then I could believe it. Before moving to this town in Missouri, I did some personal internet research and discovered that the town's race population was forty percent blacks, forty percent whites with the rest considered as "others." As I recall…I was coming from a diverse American experience of living in a small valley town in Southern California with wide racial diversity, comprising mostly Hispanics, Asians, Whites, Africans and Black Americans who seemed to relate with one another so well that no one ever made me feel black.

I was relocating to work for a privately-owned healthcare company, which had a large territory to cover in Missouri and Illinois. I had been working for a little over a year, and the team I was joining consisted of three pleasant black Americans, who had

18

been with the organization for a while. I felt right at home, as they welcomed me with open arms and treated me kindly.

Here is how the first incident occurred. I remember traveling out deep into Missouri; the team we joined was understaffed so corporate sent some help. It was a white lady who was sweet and kind, but I also take it she had been with the company for a short time. Whenever the company sent help from out of state, they were considered as "floaters."

On this particular day, in the deep of Missouri, a team of four black technicians and one white woman ventured out for work, during working hours, with each technician having a specific job. It was a busy day, and the floater happened to be very slow. We tried helping her as much as we could so she could get the hang of it, but there was only so much we could physically do as the test itself required her expertise.

The waiting room was packed like a can of sardines, and most of the people that used these services were the local farmers. I was waiting for my next patient, while the other technicians were mingling at the registration table, when a very tall *white* man in denim overalls stood and hollered as he walked out, "They need to send these goddamn Niggers' back to St Louis."

What had we done to him? The test he was waiting for was the one done by the white technician, he knew that! We had already done his testing, in which he clearly knew as we were divided by rooms, unless his eyes were that easily deceived!

I was frozen in place, mainly because I thought I didn't hear what I thought I heard. I wanted to *unhear* it. After a moment of shock and mental rewinding, I glanced over to the registration table where the other three black technicians were. Two of them were above fifty-five years old. As a matter of fact, the registration person was a retired teacher with multiple graduate degrees, and the other was a tech who had been in the healthcare industry for years, most likely even longer than my age. I knew this incident bothered the two older black co-workers more. One of them expressed their anger to me, her eyes rimmed with a thin layer of tears, as she vented her frustration.

She talked about how she'd grown up around this "mess," and how everywhere you went as a black person in America, it followed you. I felt her pain. As a person whose background wasn't exposed to this "mess," I just grappled with the question "why?" What would drive a grown man to shout out such hurtful words to people that didn't offend him in anyway?

He was just a product of his environment, right? Wrong! Clearly, there was something wrong with him and that entire waiting room.

Amazingly enough, my smart father had expressed concern over my relocation to the Mid-West (a part of me thinks I should've listened), but at the same time, had I listened, I would've remained in my naive "sunken" place of denial about the existence of racism. So, suffice it to say; *everything happens for a reason.*

I mentioned earlier that the staffing help sent in by this privately-owned healthcare company are called floaters. Floaters usually had a one to two-week assignment, while the Human Resources department worked to fill in the positions on the team, as the company "floated" people out. They also had a set of policies aligned with this; the floaters where one hundred percent responsible for taking care of their own food, and rides from the airport to the hotel. However, if a team member volunteered to pick them up and drop them off, they could claim the time. The floater always received the team's cellphone number and email address to reach the manager or assistant manager on that team. My point? Floaters had a responsibility.

On a separate incident: This was Sunday, and I hadn't heard from our floater. There were no emails, and no missed calls on the team cell phone. I drove to the hotel that she would be staying and left a message at the front desk concerning the time we would pick her up, along with my personal cell phone number, just so there wouldn't be any miscommunication. I left the hotel and headed home.

I had received her itinerary—as well and also because I was the Assistant Manager (and only management available), which showed that her flight was due to arrive at 9:55pm (I could never forget it!) By 9pm, I still hadn't heard from her. I typically went to bed early, feeling secure since I'd left a message she could receive at check-in.

The next day, I drove to the hotel to pick her up first, then head to the meeting point to pick the rest of the team. As I pulled up and she got in the van, I said, "Good morning, I am so-and-so."

21

She clicked her seat belt, and without returning my greeting or offering an introduction, she simply launched into a tirade on how she didn't eat, didn't have the van and all of that. These were complaints that floaters were not really allowed to have. It wasn't even my responsibility to feed her. The rest of the ride was quiet. I picked up the team, and they introduced themselves, still without a response from her. Seriously?

Lest I forget, she was a white Clinician (yes, I placed race in this sentence). We got to our work site and found ourselves in the same situation as with the previous floater; she was slow too, and we tried to help her as much as we could except on the physical test. I couldn't relieve her with it (the actual test) because I hadn't been trained in that task—yet. So, once again, it was all on her to do. At the end of the day, she flounced over to my station and pointed her index finger at me as she started stating all her frustrations, and how she didn't eat.

Never mind the fact that her hotel sat in the midst of a variety of restaurants, and not to mention that she could have ordered take out. Either way, it was her responsibility to figure it out, especially after being with the organization for over ten years. I had floated out too, and I always figured it out. My other co-workers were listening incredulously in the background as she carried on. She was unbelievable.

The next day, I arrived at her hotel to pick her up, but she wasn't outside. I called her room, and there was no answer. I waited for about ten minutes, all the while trying to call her. I

22

called Susan, my boss at that time, and told her that I was leaving. She gave me the go-ahead to leave, the floater's frustrations from the day before—seemed evident I wanted to make sure she was okay. Susan confirmed that I was in alignment with the company policies, and I left the hotel thereafter. That evening after work, I heard that this floater simply returned home to the state of Georgia. She did not fulfill her weeks' worth of assignments according to company policies.

That week, I received an email from the Vice President of HR telling me I needed to send this lady a letter of apology. I was utterly confused, but the concept of racism or prejudice still hadn't occurred to me (in my thought pattern—of course). I begged to differ with Dawn, the Vice President of HR (Human Resources) and stated that I did not owe this lady any apology, as I did nothing wrong. She was, in fact, the one with unnecessary discontentment, yet he insisted that I consider an apology.

When I think back on this incident, now that my eyes have been flung open, I realize what was going on. I was too naïve at that time, but at least not dumb enough to take the fall for something I clearly didn't do. Since I have been in the Mid-West, I have had fingers in my face. I have been yelled at. One white lady yelled at me, accusing me of having an attitude.

I found this to be prejudice, as I had never given her any attitude, but because my skin tone was dark, then perhaps to her, I simply had an attitude. Meanwhile, here is a kicker; I hadn't even spoken to her! Yep, I promise you, she lashed at me without me even opening my mouth. This further confirmed that my skin tone was involved for sure. I quickly realized what black America was talking about.

As a black implant to America, I find it very disheartening as I live within the world of the "accused" that white people would rather form opinions or thoughts around mere perceptions without even taking a moment to really get to know about any other race. For example, when this "white" lady lashed out at me—at work and accused me of having an attitude, I was a manager and usually "the only black employee" on the team at most times. On this occasion, I was actually speaking with another employee who happened to be a young black man we hired for a special position we were trying out.

I was simply conversing with Tony about the day's events when one of the employees that the entire team (including the lady that yelled at me—we'll call her Laura) knew as a drama queen, she was known for over-exaggerating and everyone on the team knew she popped pills—I saw it with my own eyes! (White-privilege), So…home-girl storms off "apparently" to the back from the area in which Tony and I where…my speculation is she might have tried to say something and or maybe Tony and I laughing might have worked a nerve! I don't know till this day, all I know is I didn't hear anything from her mouth.

By the time I traced Tony's eyes I noticed he was looking at her and at this time she was walking towards the back to join the other Clinicians. (Lord-knows-what-was-said-once-she-got-there), the next thing I knew is this lady "Laura" who I had worked together with in harmony (so I thought for over five years), came from around the corner (looking pissed-off), her face was red as a tomato, concerned about her (as I usually was) I followed her in the direction she was going. I had to holler to get her attention because I thought something was wrong with her family member or someone in the back had upset her (honestly), once I asked her if she was ok.

She came hard at me—index finger in my face and all (honey! She called me all kinds of things but a Monkey, Ape and the N—word) truthfully…it wouldn't have mattered, I was hurt (not because my emotions are unstable) but because I had worked alongside this individual all these years, stood up for her—never said a bad thing about her and was loyal to her only to find out that she trusted an employee who was not only new but, she-Laura knew this girls madness! She's the one that always highlighted it! (Really?) All based on what the "junkie" had said or is it because she is white and I am black—I don't know America?

But as a black person this is the quandary. You tell me? What would you think? After our working relationship wouldn't you think it would have been better and easier to approach me and say; "Hey. So-and-so claims this—what's going on?" She could have just claimed that she wanted clarity because at the end of the day; I don't know what lies so-and-so went back there and said, I tried my best not to look at it like a black and white issue but when you've had someone's back for so long and you realize when stuff hits the fan you're on an island by yourself (race before loyalty!)

White people…I am not going to lie, that left me feeling some type of way. I saw and experienced with my own being that a white person will go to back for another white person (even knowing the other-white persons deceptive reputation) before they even consider going to back for a black person—they personally know. The problem with black people is; black people (are too loyal) and because black people coined *"I-got-yo-back"* meant; Loyalty, that's imbedded in our DNA from the tribes in Africa, we are protectors and once we trust and are loyal—we are there full throttle! Yes, everyone on the team knew she (the girl that started the mess) popped pills, but maybe because she was white, it was okay, wasn't it?!

What I found ironic was the fact that Laura had known me longer than she knew any of these employees (meaning I was approachable and we'd shared lots of carpooling time together etc.) We had worked together for years on the same team and never had I ever given her any attitude. But apparently, the day another white girl tells her something about me and or Tony and me? She became a different person.

Even though she should've known my character. Wow! I don't know, America…this is where I grapple with my reality. I want to call this prejudice or even racist but, maybe that's because I don't have any other choice words that encapsulate betrayal. How is one supposed to look at it? You knew me for over five years, yet this one time you literally yell at me over something that was said by another "white" person? (I am not stupid. She took that moment to get all that little-feeling build up that she was holding back come out…I don't know what else to think). I was just shocked because I have never done anything wrong to her on purpose.

Even Tony was in disbelief. He couldn't believe that she could yell at me like that, with her finger in my face. And to think I was supposedly her boss. The organizational chart required that she report to me as a Manager. Now imagine if the tables were turned? If a black person went off on their boss with their index finger in their face...never mind, I won't hold my breath for that response. I just need America to explain to me how this works? In case you are wondering what I was doing while I was being yelled at. I was in shock and automatically apologizing (because I cared for this lady and didn't want to see her upset), because this lady was the same age as my own mother, and if there was anything I knew, it was never to disrespect older people. Heck! I don't even give my own *mama* an attitude (as old as I am—today I still fear and respect that lady).

The everyday reality 6

"Our true nationality is mankind." –H.G. Wells

It bothers me so much that some people can choose to treat you a certain way simply because of the color of your skin. That still doesn't resonate with me. I am trying to wrap my mind around it, and I am just at a loss. I got to the point where I was trying not to look at everything as "white" and "black," because I feared it might force me to become the person I most resent…the "racist." Yet, I wonder how I can then accurately dissect these issues and process them rationally without becoming that person. For instance, when we consider the senseless police shootings, one party says "they were doing their job," and the other party insists that "black skin is being hunted."

I cannot seem to understand how these issues work. I know I am under qualified to have a valid opinion as I do not have the full black American experience, but honey, this little experience is enough to see right through the bull. When I try to rationalize the shootings, I just can't help but wonder how they can successfully "arrest" mass shooters like Dylan Roof with no scratches. "They" tried to say that the young black man in Louisiana had a gun in his pocket, and the officers were seen on top of him in the video, yet

28

people like Dylan Roof were simply called in for having "guns" that's with an "S!" Help me understand—America? I am trying to rationalize and not get on anyone's bandwagon, but you can't conceal the truth… not when it's in plain sight.

Sure, the cops that arrested Dylan Roof are not the same as the killer ones, but do they not all get the same training on handling all people with "guns?"

There is a plethora of stories that can be dissected and placed in the courts of personal opinion, yet as an outsider looking in, I can still say that something smells fishy. And trust me, I am the first one to be the last one to look for racial incidences, but America, how does one process situations like the Starbucks incident? When the news broke all over social media, I remember telling my husband that I wanted to see a video first. When the video came out, I was mortified. I feel like the more I try to justify, or perhaps, deny the truth, the more the boldface truth stares me down. Don't get me wrong… I'm not saying that I do not believe racism doesn't exist. Oh, it does! My denial is my mind's way of trying to find the beauty within the red, blue and white flag.

This is America! Most foreigners would trade places with anyone in America any day, but unbeknownst to unsuspecting minors or black foreigners, the truth lies just beneath the surface. Yes, she is gorgeous as hell! She is America, powerful… the place to be and do what you desire. But don't get carried away, it's not all fun and games. I know that no country is perfect. But the racism here is sickening. I have mentally taken stock and tried to reconcile all the inconsistent stories being flung at me every day, both on a national and personal level.

Then the Starbucks event happened. Don't get me wrong, I have been gravely affected by the obvious injustices on blacks, especially our men, but watching the video of those two young men from the beginning to the point where they got escorted out in handcuffs raised new emotions in me.

I guess that's also because I am getting older and I feel like these kids could've been my sons. I have nephews and a few nieces here in the U.S., and all of that flashed through my mind and caused me to ask, "When is this going to stop, America?" I don't get it. Black Americans didn't ask to be here in the first place. They are here making the best of being displaced already. You think Alkebulan (Mother of mankind) wanted her children stolen from her in such a manner? Being in the Mid-West has been both a blessing and a curse, but everything happens for a reason and a season. I am ready to move back to the west coast for the sake of diversity.

I know that had I not experienced this life, I would have remained naïve and in denial of the white and black prejudices. One of the best experiences in the Mid-West is the larger demographic of blacks, it tends to remind me of home…Africa.

I have drawn knowledge and great wisdom from my brothers and sisters. For instance, I still marvel at the fact that African Americans have to have a talk with their sons about law enforcement. What conversations are white Americans having with their sons about survival? For the longest time, I've wondered why most black people lived within the same regions. It makes sense now. After working for a travel company, I found it interesting that white Americans can practically live anywhere they want—in America, even in the middle of nowhere. I've met tons of people that brag about their neighbors being about miles away! How sweet. But I know for a fact that it is not the same for black people.

The closer together they settle, the safer they feel…safety in numbers! It's interesting how there is such a parallel difference back home in my country of birth, where blacks can live anywhere they choose…freely! My grandmothers lived out in rural settlements far from most people, which made for a serene environment and relaxing visits.

However, the reality of black people in America is that though they are "free" from slavery, they cannot live wherever they want. Some can dare to, but we all know how that situation can easily escalate, so why even try? The realities are that when we go job hunting or work in places that are not so racially diverse, we tend to feel like we are walking on egg-shells. I really do wish that corporate diversity training would be mandatory for every single organization.

I get that sometimes, some of you haven't been in such close proximity with a black person, let alone one that is heavily colored but please, stop with the hair questions. You and I know that black women are going to switch up their hairstyles quite often, and most times it can actually be coming out of a pack. No one feels like being your "urban class 101." And when we exasperatedly choose to give you one-word answers, then we have an attitude. But do we ask you how often you wash your hair? Exactly!

Let me talk about the workforce; I could write a whole chapter on this. Attention, white America! The fact that black people may choose not to smile at you or talk to you does not mean they have an issue with you. There has been so many times that I felt like I had to fake a smile when all I really wanted to do was be left in my own headspace. Alas, when I didn't smile, the white women around me would ask if everything was fine or if they offended me. It's actually annoying. I get that you all like to smile, but that's not how it always works with black folk. The current perception is that a black girl would naturally have an attitude or just be angry, but why can't it be that she's just confident, and being a boss-lady going about her business?

That's all I wanted to do… be serious be in my zone. It's not my fault that my confidence is intimidating, and I just know what I want out of life. We just keep it real, and honesty or directness should not be taken as being rude. You don't need a smile from any black person to make you feel "safe." My experience so far is that it's scary and uncomfortable being black in America.

Life here considers me black because my skin speaks first, not my accent, and certainly not my nationality; therefore, I am one of the targets. This doesn't make me feel at ease. I've often told my husband who is African American, that I have a lot of respect for him and his people. I haven't lived here all my life, but for the period that I have, I've felt like an unwelcome guest, especially in the Mid-West. It's unreal how a group of people have to fight and protest to prove that they also "matter" as human beings, and even when they do, it's always misconstrued.

Black vs. White 7

"The best way to stop discrimination on the basis of race is to stop discriminating on the basis of race." –John Roberts

Often times a "normalized" dysfunction is interrupted by strangers or outsiders. For instance, if the children in a certain family have lived all their lives adhering to crazy, militant and radical rules laid down by their parents. All they are accustomed to is this life with their parents; After all, they've never lived another life for a long period of time at anyone else's house.

One day, long-lost aunt Gertrude visits them, stays for a month, and realizes that something is just weird in the family within that period. In spite of the fact that she is only a relative to one of the parents, she can see right through the mess and realizes how ridiculous the lifestyle in that household is. She knows it's like that because of the way they were raised, and even though she chose a different path for herself, it appears that her sibling (one of the parents) chose to continue the tradition their own parents created for them. Well, America, I am just an outsider looking in…

and living in it as well, and trust me, I had no choice.
The adults in my life made the migration choice, for which I am really grateful, but that being said, I sometimes feel that you have to be out of the dysfunction to know what's real, what's normal and what's absurd.

I don't claim to have been born in paradise, but I do know that my place of birth gave me a naivety to race and pride of blackness that I wouldn't have otherwise known or understood if it wasn't for the migration. Up till now, I still literally have a hard time believing that someone is racist. I might think it, or maybe even utter it in a group conversation, but my heart is never quite convinced, and I really don't know why. I figure a larger portion of this stems from never really growing up in that environment (in which the oppressors still persecute a people).

I wonder if white people in America could ever see black people in America in a different light since this prejudice appears to be all they've ever known? Please understand that I am not trying to make excuses or justify the white attitude. It's just one of those situations in which I try to figure things out and expect it to make sense.

Dear Black People 8

"Never be limited by other people's limited imaginations."
—Dr. Mae Jemison

Everything is not racially influenced. We need to learn as a people to halt, gather all the facts and then decide on how best to act on them. I'll explain. As a black team leader one year, we happened to have a diverse mix of staff on the team. I had been working with this company for about thirteen years, and I knew how things worked. Naturally, as a leader, there were weak aspects of their performances that caught my attention. I wanted to address their mistakes and keep them out of trouble.

I could easily have decided not to say anything on the assumption that they should know how the work industry runs. But I chose to offer guidance, and even though I couldn't go into much detail because they were not in leadership, I used subliminal language. I remember telling them to identify their job descriptions, focus on it and master it so that no one would breathe down their necks. There was even a white lady on the team who struggled a little but ensured that she didn't make any mistakes that alerted corporate.

One of the *sistas* (not sist—er) said, "Oh, so X, the white lady struggles, but we are the ones being scolded." Right there, I learned something shocking. I stopped her in her tracks and had to reiterate that this was not a black and white issue. What they were struggling with was basic and pivotal to their clinical work. The funny thing was that the "white" woman she was referring to wasn't making huge mistakes that could potentially get the company sued, they were! That was why I was trying to gently call them to order, yet my being equally black did not stop them from feeling that a "white" person was being favored…so much that they could not see that I was trying to help them out!

I said all that to say this; not everything in life, black America, is racially infused. The reason I think I've held on to the idea of gathering all the facts before drawing a conclusion is simply that I know the devil has the ability to trick one's mind into seeing something that really isn't there. I'd rather process things rationally and decipher the truth. We cannot go around calling everything black and white…it causes our opinions to lose value and truth, thereby losing proper public consideration. No one will take us seriously if we constantly postulate white-on-black crime theories.

Not all white people are racist or prejudiced, and some of us get that. For those who don't, please do not lump all white people in the same category. The same follows with this book; my general use of the word white does not mean I believe that all white people in America are the same.

Dear black people, not everything is black culture. Who died and made us the judges of culture appropriateness anyway? It's embarrassing to me when I read "black twitter" going in on people like Bruno Mars. We must understand that it's a privilege to have people emulate what we call "black culture." Back home in Africa, all I did was spend time watching black American movies and music videos trying to emulate them.

I remember when Aaliyah came out on the scene, I loved her look; Joe Boxers showing underneath baggy pants, baggy plaid shirt, bandana and flat ironed hair with super long boots… I literally begged my mother to buy me some "Dr Martens" (they were not knee high, but they were *dope!*) Because of Aaliyah. I wanted to dress like the chocolate version of Aaliyah, and when Da Brat came out (Girl! Shut-the-front-door!) I was heavily rocking two strand twists and all the outfits (and low-key I thought I could spit mean bars *Lyrics* too!) *Excuse me as I laugh at myself*…that's the only reason I watched African American movies and music videos, on VHS, might I add…so I could be hip—to the game.

It hurt me immensely when we moved to America and I started high school, the black American students were not warm towards me. They were in a sense mean. They made fun of me, my accent and Africa, which is quite laughable because we actually share those roots. I had girls wanting to fight me over nothing.

Yet you want to ask Africans, *"how come Y'all don't like us?"* In any case, that's a lie, most Africans I know want to emulate the black western culture. Let's learn to decipher the lies that have been created to divide us as a people. I spent my entire high school experience hanging out with African students and one African American student that didn't mind our company.

If people want to emulate the "black culture," let them. It's not your personal franchise. Instead, you should feel a sense of pride. We are so quick to get upset over nothing. Think about this; what other culture is emulated around the world? (I'll wait…) Yes! The answer is black American! From Japan to the Horn of Africa, everyone is somehow trying to be like you. Who says blacks are not influential?

If we want to be treated a certain way, we have to treat others in the same way. It begins with us. I was annoyed on how some black Americans where socially treating Amara La Negra (my sister called me to tell me about this reality star and singer), who I think is a very beautiful, exotic epitome of blackness. It reminded me of the time when I came to America and realized that though we have the same skin tone, we are not deemed black enough because of our accents. Black is black! Period! Black doesn't have to sound like you. At a certain point in my life, I became insecure being around black Americans…I would refuse to talk because of my accent. When I tried to talk like an American, they said I sounded white. I just couldn't win! I finally got rid of the "thick accent," and now, I sounded "white." Wow!

I tried speaking in *"Ebonics,"* which proved to be a total disaster. My best friend from my home country told me to stop, my brother said I sounded like a valley girl trying too hard to sound "black," and my father red flagged me! He claimed I was speaking "broken English" so I had to go back to my African-valley-girl-sounding-self and just figured I wouldn't talk much around black Americans so I wouldn't draw attention to myself.

One of the things I liked about the Mid-West; once in a blue moon, I would have that one black person that was almost on to me, but it wasn't obvious! Black Americans in the Mid-West in my opinion, tended to be more friendly, warm and very hospitable. I loved the Mid-West because of this (feeling of warmth I received from like people), but I truly despised its scarcity of diversity that made my skin that much more noticeable to the ones that didn't care for blacks.

I believe it's time to embrace everyone with open arms. Let's be the change agents we so desperately seek. If Rachel Dolezal, who is an amazing artist, by the way, wants to be black, we should embrace her. She knows her own truth. Who are we to judge and castigate her? Being black is such a privilege! We might not feel like we live in privilege in America, but what other race is so copied, capitalized on talent and or duplicated?! That's why I am excited about my Melanin. We can go anywhere, choose to blend in and not be messed with.

I always encourage black Americans to visit other countries, especially Africa, if you can. Go to Europe or South America. I want you to experience the amazing hospitality you can enjoy in other countries. You are the kings and queens, stolen from lucrative villages that were prosperous. Trust and believe that Alkebulan (Mother of mankind) was rich and still is.

The narrative has to change. The seed of deception was placed in your hearts from the very beginning. Black America; where are the names of the chiefs that sold your ancestors? Of course, the records of ship captains and pioneers can be provided (and…we are accountable for Christopher Columbus but not the chiefs names, village names, tribes and or locations—nothing in specific?) If a race can openly deny stealing another race from its native kingdom, then there is nothing left to prove. We already know the truth. Nowadays, science itself has caught up to us, what are the "Genealogy" tests claiming when it comes to the percentage of African DNA found in Caucasians? (The truth— might I add. But! Let's carry on….)

Damage control 101 in western books, is to say and believe the weak line; *"Y'all sold one another,"* as the reason why black people are divided. Who sells a car without the vehicles papers such as registration of the car and title? Well, a person selling a stolen car…that's who. We cannot be productive as a people as long as there is division. I earnestly dream of a day that we'll come together all over the world.

Our purpose is greater than the narrative that's been told to us, and we need to start declaring to our children, a narrative of power, resistance—against our own insecurities as a race, and freedom. The enslaved ancestors did not take a beating so the youth of this country could end up killing one other. Alkebulan (Mother of mankind) wants her sons and daughters to rise up in victory!

Dear White People 9

"Hardly any aspect of my life, from where I had lived, to my education, to my employment history, to my friendships, had been free from the taint of racial inequity, from racism, from whiteness. My racial identity had shaped me from the womb forward. I had not been in control of my own narrative. It wasn't just race that was a social construct. So was I." — Tim Wise, White Like Me

Dear white people (at least, some of you), why is it easier for you to dismiss and deflect black America's experiences? I wonder if its heritage guilt or generational tendencies. You must realize (for me—specifically) as Africans, the story of our people (in my African Country) and how the British stole our land has been passed from generation to generation—forever etched in our memories and stamped on the pages of our hearts. Whether I wanted to know it or not, whether the history books were western or not, our ancestors made sure that as decedents of King Mwenemutapa, we were told what happened. This recycled information is what I will pass on to the next generation as well.

Therefore, I say all that to say; no matter how much we want to sweep things under the rug—in America, black generations to come will always know about their people and the slave trade that ruined their world, especially with today's technology.

So, while the white supremacist aims to "preserve" his race, and every other non-black aims to live in denial, black folks all around the world are awakening. The way I see it, we are all human beings, and we might as well learn to co-exist peacefully now and set better precedence for the coming generations because all these irreconcilable differences will be a mess for our kids to clean up.

It's true that black people understand that you are not "the ones" that brought their ancestors into bondage, as do they know that they are not who their ancestors were, but I can certainly say that they don't feel as free as non-blacks have felt. This is why most (not all) black Americans don't care much for the slogan "Make America Great Again:" There's never been a "great" moment in their history, as the laws of this nation have NEVER been pro-black. So, please understand that white people in America have no reason to feel guilty or defensive about "race" issues. Black people are not here to blame you for the current situation, they just want to be acknowledged as human beings along with their feelings, experiences, and they also want to feel safe in a land that their forefathers literally built.

(For free, might I add), is it too much to ask that black people begin to feel an equal treatment with white people? We don't want what you have; we just want to coexist equally. It's never been a power tussle on my end or that of the other black people close to me. Of course, I can't speak for the other end consisting of the white supremacists, Neo-Nazis, the KKK and so forth, because I am still confused about their agenda. No disrespect, but I have

really tried but failed to get it, so I just stay out of their way.
It still gets pretty confusing how the goal is "white" preservation,
yet they love "Jesus" and hate "Jews." Anyway, I digress. I just
want to live like you…breathe, get up, go about my business and
not "worry about it being my last day." Before all of this, I was
never a "worry warrior," but I would be lying if I didn't say my
heart skips a beat these days, when a cop car is behind me (Yes!
Even in my German luxury fully loaded engineered car) I know
everything is legit, insurance is current, Driver's license is current,
hey, I even have two forms of Identification just to avoid any
problems. I know the cops behind me are running my plates, but I
hate the feeling of having someone pull you over "just" to mess
with you.

Dear white people, that's obviously not a thing for you, but
believe me, that's what's going on in my mind when cops show up
behind me, and I hate it. I have literally even gotten into the habit
of grabbing my phone and placing it in between my hands,
standing ready for whatever. This is the West! I am not a paranoid
person, I'm "just" cautious. I have "just" seen enough reality to
know that anything is possible when driving "while black" in
America. After all, what do you say when a person feels that they
are doing everything they need to do as a Citizen that's in the law,
and in 2018, a 65-year-old black woman still gets manhandled
aggressively by four white cops while another arrives on the scene.
She screams as she's being shackled, and video surveillance did
not show any signs of resistance from her end.

What about a black graduate in an Ivy League school? She (the black student) fell asleep in the common study area, whose white "school colleague" walked over to her to just to tell her she will be calling the cops on her. Why couldn't she (the white student) just say, "Hey! Checking in on you…looks like you dozed off." After all, America, these two were neighbors.

What about the Black man who was freely barbecuing in the Oakland Park, at which a random white woman decided to make it her business to call the cops…because he (the black-dude) was using the "wrong" grill. By the way, this woman was not a park ranger or an employee of the city.

She just woke up that morning and thought, "I'm going to ignore everyone else in the park that's barbequing, and I will target the black man and… oh, forget all the world's problems, let's just go mess up someone else's day." Unbelievable! This incident was very interesting to me; not only was she the aggressor in this incident, when the police finally pulled up, she also became the victim! Cowering in crocodile tears, she was acting like she was utterly distraught as if she had been running from danger. Yet, no one had asked her to police anyone.

I need to take a brief pause here, to point out my share of these experiences as I talk about the said lady in the Oakland Park incident. I am reminded of the times in my own life where I was attacked, three times to be precise, with "white woman tears." (Yes, there is such a weapon in America.) I often mention to my black American husband how I think black people have endured the most irritating white behavior, for the longest time. I don't know how y'all do it (black Americans—that is).

You should have seen this lady's behavior; she went from being this authoritative I-own-the-park-so-you-will-do-it-my-way attitude with an aggressive tone, to a "weeping victim" by the time the cops showed up. You have to see this video on YouTube, its real! I served as a leader on a predominately white team; I was the only black person most of the time. The first time I experienced the Oakland-type tears, a lady I had known for years lashed out at me. I had done absolutely nothing to deserve it.

And that's the other thing white people, while we are on this subject, if some of you would simply speak your mind each time you need to, you wouldn't hold back all your frustration only to dump it all on us once you're having a bad day. Stop giving forced smiles like everything is okay. I see through the smiles anyway.

Back to my story, this woman lashed out at me, index finger in my face, and told me I had an attitude. I later realized what that meant; I hadn't conversed with her that morning other than a standard cordial greeting, and that morning my vibrational waves were at a positive ten. Anyway, it was all about her feelings, plus a healthy helping of the white woman tears, so, I inevitably apologized because whatever the case may have been, she was crying. (Right?)

The second time, I believe she misconstrued a business memorandum, and instead of approaching me (whom she had known and worked with for a very long time), she called our boss, who called to tell me that she was distraught because she thought the business MEMO was about her and her daughter.

By the way, this was now years after the first incident. I was confused…how does one person out of an entire group of employees feel personally attacked? What's up with that, white America? Guilty? So, this meant that not only could I not do my job, I was also expected to walk on eggshells because a fifty-five-year-old lady who was the exact same age as my mother, felt that I had nothing better to do than to spend my time plotting against her and her daughter? Wow! White America, some of you have to do better. The worst part of it was that even my own boss who knew me and was familiar with my character couldn't hear me out on the issue. This was a man I thought was business savvy, yet he had been bought by the "white woman tears." I often wonder, white women, what have black women done to you? Because as far as I know, I don't want your men, I don't want your life, I don't even for a second want to be you.

I just want to live comfortably and confidently in my skin, and not be judged as having an attitude just because I don't feel like putting on a fake smile like some of you. And if we're really honest, you want us to smile at you so you can feel less "threatened," but we have never been threatening.

The third incident happened at the hands of a fifty-eight-year-old woman. Needless to say, she managed to single-handedly destroy everything I had worked so hard to build, but she never broke my character or my spirit. Through her, I learned how evil people could be and extremely resentful of this black skin. I am just glad that I am a strong person. I "just" can't comprehend why black skin bothers some white people. I'll never get it.

Moving on as we dissect the incidences so far in 2018, I am drawn to the two black investors in the Philadelphia Starbucks. Theirs was just a model of the narrative of black people thinking that if they just did what they were supposed to, they'll draw less attention to themselves, only for white America to keep reminding them otherwise. So far, we also have a sixty-five-year-old lady in Georgia (someone's mother or grandmother), a Yale Graduate student, two investors and the lanky black boy who was taking his sister to prom who was being choked by some big ol' husky cop. The ironic part is that "they" claim he was resisting arrest. Well, America, I would like to see anyone else who would give full compliance while they are getting choked.

When a human being gets provoked or feels threatened, we go intuitively into survival mode. I have watched the video repeatedly. When the cop slammed the young black man against the glass, his hands were already in the air. However, when the cop started choking him, the young man switched to survival mode. When I speak of cops, I am also aware that there are "some" black cops that use aggressive force, most times the black community is not against authority and or saying authority is "parse" racist the numbers reveal blacks are at a higher percentage of being mishandled in the hands of officers (now that I got that out the way). Let's talk about that time a black man legitimately had a permit and a weapon. He tried to tell the officer, but before he could get his sentence out, the officer shot numerous times into the vehicle, with a child and the driver's fiancée still inside.

The examples span from way back till now. There are a million other examples that don't just illustrate police brutality, but that also depict injustices that are felt by black people from college to the corporate platform.

I almost feel like you'd be naïve as a black person in America to think it would never happen to you. I am not trying to create paranoia, it's just living in reality. I used to feel the exact same way. I'd always make sure my tags were not expired, and always drive an updated car so I don't have to worry about mechanical issues. I'd make sure my car insurance was always full coverage and maximum on everything…set on Autopay. I'd make sure that I crossed all my "T's and dotted all my "I's," and assume I shouldn't have any "cop" problems. But now I know better.

Once again, I can't represent all black Americans, but I have observed that those who have any sense at all, know that you are not directly responsible for what your ancestors did. The Black American race just wants to co-exist and be acknowledged as equal human beings. This can simply be done by considering their feelings and emotions. I have noticed that when black America voices any injustice, white America is quick to deflect their pain and dismiss their feelings, and most times even rob them of the authenticity of their experiences. Yet, you wonder why there are angry black Americans. They might be "free" from slavery, but they are still tied into enslaved institutions. I may be a foreigner, but I can see right through the bull!

Let's talk about Colin Kaepernick and the white-media-slaughter. Would it have hurt any white journalist(s) or white people if they simply reached out to the man and asked him why he was kneeling, before burning jerseys and speaking about something they knew nothing of? This was simple, even for me. Dude took a knee in protest...personal protest. So, how did White America twist it to fit the narrative of him protesting the flag? Please help me understand that part? They sing the national anthem with hands placed on the left side, and I know there was a flag being flown in the background, but Colin wasn't personally responsible for holding it, was he?

So why did white America throw the disrespect of the flag in the mix? With the flag came the troops? Seriously? I don't know Kaepernick from Adam, but his personal mission was simple. I am not picking a side. I just want to understand why when a black football player takes a knee, he is disrespecting a flag that he wasn't holding and the troops, but when Tim Tebow (white football player) did it, he was not castigated. Oh, I know...because everyone knew he was praying since we all had communication with him?

That was not what Tim's team was doing, and it could still be considered offensive by another group of people, right? How about the little black boy with the monkey branded on his shirt? The comments on the Facebook posts left me disgusted. Truth is, if you have never been black a day in your life in America, you cannot speak, dismiss, relate or deflect the black American Experience. The issues are real!

Black Americans are still silenced by deflection and dismissal, just like when they had no rights in the days of slavery. If you are a black woman and you are in America's feminist groups, ask yourself the last time they marched for your rights? I don't even have to elaborate on this one.

The young real estate investors that were unjustly arrested at Starbucks after being there for two minutes were dismissed as "trespassing" by a white YouTuber. I just shook my head at his pathetic seven-minute video. He felt that they broke the "law," perhaps the same "law" that allowed the lynching and killing of Negros back in the day? It's this kind of dangerous thinking that continually keeps the black race under emotional neglect. This was what Black America was always trying to tell me; clear as day, in a public shop, they had been dismissed as "trespassing," yet a white witness stated she had waited for her son in that same Starbucks for an hour and even used the bathroom without buying anything. After this, I knew for sure that we are still far from crossing the bridge of racism in America.

After watching some documentaries and trying to figure out what's going on with the white supremacy, all I can say from my observation is that we don't want what you want and I'm not even sure, where that notion came from. I've repeatedly heard most white supremacist groups state that we "blacks" want to take over.

No one wants to take over anything. We just want to live in peace, along with our loved ones, that's it! We want to co-exist in the same country, and not think about being hunted like wild animals.

We don't want anything from any race. You don't owe us anything, and we don't owe you anything. I am not qualified to speak on reparations, as this might be something ongoing, but we want to add to society fairly like all other races and raise our children to attain and aspire to the same things as other races. We don't want to continue to give our male children talks about encounters with law enforcement, because even that sometimes doesn't work. Philando Castile got murdered telling an officer he had a permit to carry the weapon on him. Let's just start by being allowed to survive in America!

I can't speak for all blacks; after all, I am a transplant. But I can say that no matter how superior you consider yourself in your mind, keep it in your mind. You don't need to attempt to convince us. Most radical groups already live in the middle of nowhere in America, where no blacks exist, so there should be no basis for competition. I always bug out when I watch the Netflix Documentaries of the White Supremacists because all I pay attention to is the background which typically states, *"All whites live here."* One more thing, not all black people are the same; so, stop putting us in the same categories. We are just like you...different mentally, socially, and intellectually.

At the end of the day... 10

"The capacity for getting along with our neighbor depends to a large extent on the capacity for getting along with ourselves. The self-respecting individual will try to be as tolerant of his neighbor's shortcomings as he is of his own." —Eric Hoffer

I have noticed while working in a non-diverse workforce, that white people do a lot of speculation. They think that all they have seen or heard on television and or think among their "white clan" about black people is true. And they act on it. It's fair to say that we all have some form of prejudice (yes, blacks—too); suffice it to say, when certain white people talk to me in a certain way, I have to process the information like a computer before responding so that I don't find myself responding as though I thought they were saying something racist. I have to x-ray that person's possible intent and queries and dig deep in my heart to decipher if the source in which the message comes from is overt or pure (because I like my racism overt—fact! Be bold with it), and I believe most black people operate with this same mindset.

You can't blame me, maybe that's my prejudice, but after you have been lashed out at—for no reason and or been treated blatantly unjust—racially and or with prejudice and or even had a person tell you they are prejudice to your face I like to exercise caution. If a lady has had her purse stolen and or snatched out of

54

her hands in broad day light, she might feel violated, scared, a little traumatized, maybe paranoid and that one event might just make her very cautious in life of every person that passes her way…you get the analogy—right? That's my stand in life about white folks…I want to trust every one of you, but I have to protect myself—too.

While blacks (not all) take time to process information, it appears that whites (not all) tend to bank on speculation. It is clear that both races need to enter into honest and extensive dialogue in order to understand each other's stories and realities—we keep talking about each other among each other but not to each other.

My intention is not to write to convince one race over the other, my intention is not to blame and or find fault in any race over the other. Nor do I have the recipe to end racism and or prejudice ways. I'm simply sharing my firsthand experiences and observations, and how I have been treated based on speculation (prejudice) due to my skin tone. I also fully understand that not all non-blacks or white people are racist.

Here is my conclusion;

White people teach your children to get to know people before placing a tag and or label on certain races. We are not "they." We (black people) all represent various forms of upbringing, and I think the more people get to know another person, the more understanding you obtain, like the white race we have, Bougie *(Bourgeois)* black folks, smart black folks, rich and wealthy black folks, super-educated-articulate black folks, regular black folks, average black folks, ghetto black folks, poor black folks.

I have traveled in rural America and I have seen ghetto and super poor white folks—I'm just saying, the difference between some poor whites and blacks is the poor white American can hide in rural America in a trailer atop passed down family acreage—with a washed-up confederate flag-pole dead center of the property…hopelessly waving to its last breath (away from public's view so…no one can ever see their struggle parse) and blacks are subjected to the projects and or poor neighborhoods—that are more visible to society. We are all mainly and mostly alike than we are different, just different privileges and resources….

Black people, the truth lies in this; if we want to be treated better, then we as a people need to start treating ourselves with the utmost excellence…not for anyone, not for a show but for ourselves. You simply must act the way you want to be treated. This cannot be over-emphasized. I go into detail in my follow up book entitled: The Agenda, *Wake up! Black America now is your time.* I continue to live with the hope that eventually, all of humanity will come together and cherish, learn from and grow into one another's cultures.

Homage 11

"Art matters. It is not simply a leisure activity for the privileged or a hobby for the eccentric. It is a practical good for the world. The work of the artist is an expression of hope - it is an homage to the value of human life, and it is vital to society. Art is a sacred expression of human creativity that shares the same ontological ground as all human work. Art, along with all work is the ordering of creation toward the intention of the creator." —Michael Gungor

Indeed, it is in those that I call my ancestors, and my relatives through visceral blood lineage that I know I am who I am today. Your ways of humility, perseverance, and endurance have also been imparted into my generation, and the generations of many to come. This I have drawn from your strength; to always be myself, and live in true happiness, light, and love for all humanity. I have learned from you that everything has been a true measure of character and I know for a fact that you were able to endure discrimination, racism, and prejudices that you didn't sign up for. You remained in great and optimistic spirits, and with that same understanding, I know that I can as well. Thank you. May your spirit and life live on forever as a beacon of hope, light, and love; these are the people among many that have indirectly taught me how to navigate the West in my blackness and to take full ownership of my heritage with no apologies: King Mwenemutapa, Steve Biko, Nelson Mandela, Robert Mugabe, Ambuya Nehanda,

Malcom X, Dr. Martin Luther King, Nina Simone, Winnie Mandela, Joshua Nkomo, Shaka Zulu, Mansa Musa, Queen Makeda, Yaa Asantewa, King Lobengula, Harriet Tubman, Sojourner Truth, Rosa Parks, Langston Hughes, Phillis Wheatley, Maya Angelou, Zora Neale Hurston, W.E.B. Du Bois, Oprah Winfrey, Michelle Obama, President Barrack Obama, Iyanla Vanzent, Dr. Boyce Watkins, Michael Eric Dyson, Tim Wise and John Brown.